P9-CNC-520

Numbers Through 100

From the Read-Aloud Anthology

100 Days of School

Trudy Harris

illustrations by Beth Griffis Johnson

Access Prior Knowledge

This story will help you review

- Counting through 20
- Addition and subtraction strategies through 10

ISBN-13: 978-0-618-59091-9
ISBN-10: 0-618-59091-9
ISBN-13: 978-0-618-67179-3
ISBN-10: 0-618-67179-X

271a

17 18 19 20 21 22 23 24 25 0877 17 16 15 14 13 12   Printed in the U.S.A.
4500368901

If 10 tired children all take off
their shoes, what do you get?
Lots of bare feet!
And . . .
(I suppose)
100 toes!

If **20** children each
drop **5** papers on the
floor, what do you get?
100 papers.
And . . .
(I would guess)
an awful mess.

Name _____

Use the pictures on pages 271b and 271c.

1. How many shoes do
   5 children take off?

   _____ shoes

2. How many shoes do
   10 children take off?

   _____ shoes

3. Each child drops **5** papers.
   How many papers do **2**
   children drop altogether?

   _____ papers

4. **6** children are in a line.
   4 more children join them.
   How many children are
   there in all?

   _____ children

MATH at Home

Dear Family,

My class is starting Unit 4. I will be learning about place value, regrouping, and number patterns. I will also be learning about ordinal numbers, from first through tenth. These pages show what I will learn and have activities for us to do together.

From, _____

Vocabulary

These are some words I will use in this unit.

ones and tens In the number 25, the 2 stands for 2 tens, and the 5 stands for 5 ones.

one hundred 10 groups of 10 ones

regroup Trade 10 ones blocks for 1 tens block.

estimate You can estimate when you do not need to find the exact answer.

Some other words I will use are **odd**, **even**, **before**, **after**, and **between**.

Vocabulary Activity

Turn the page for more.

Let's work together to complete these sentences.

1. When you trade 10 ones for 1 ten you _____.

2. If you have 10 tens you have _____.

3. When you do not need to find the exact answer you can _____.

4. In the number 12, the 1 is in the _____ place, and

   the 2 is in the _____ place.

School Tools

Connect the dots.
Start at 1.
Finish at 20.

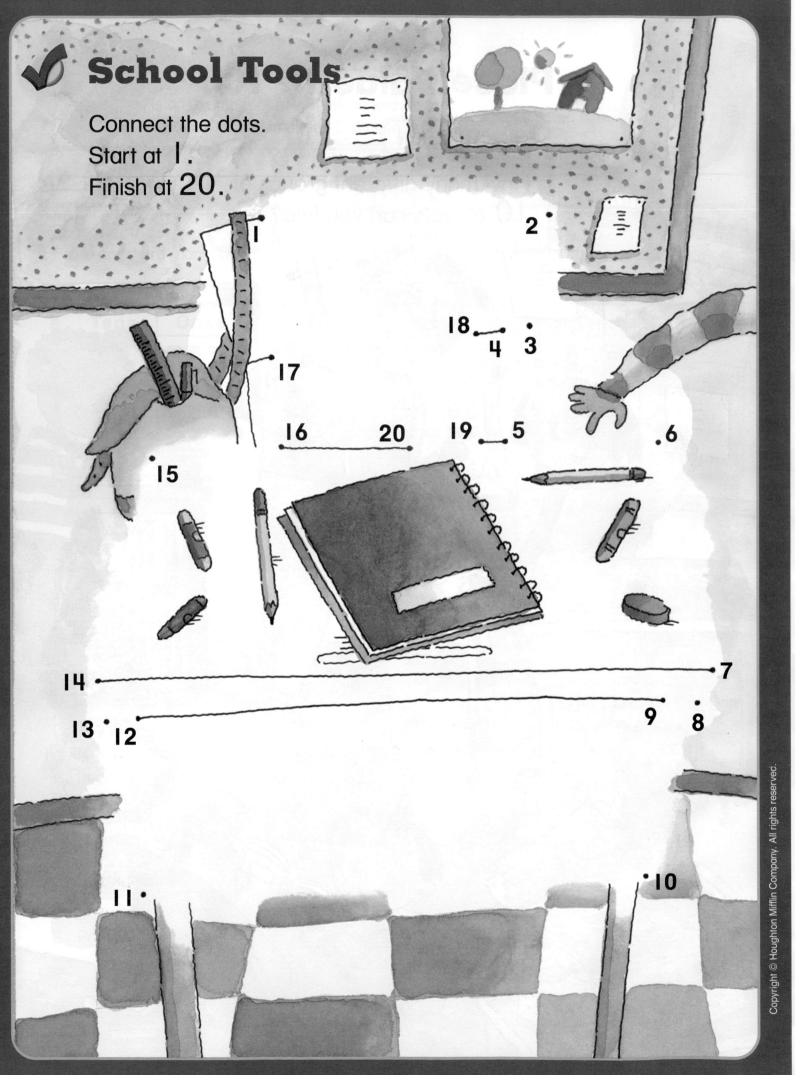

Name _____

Teen Numbers

Making groups of ten helps you count.

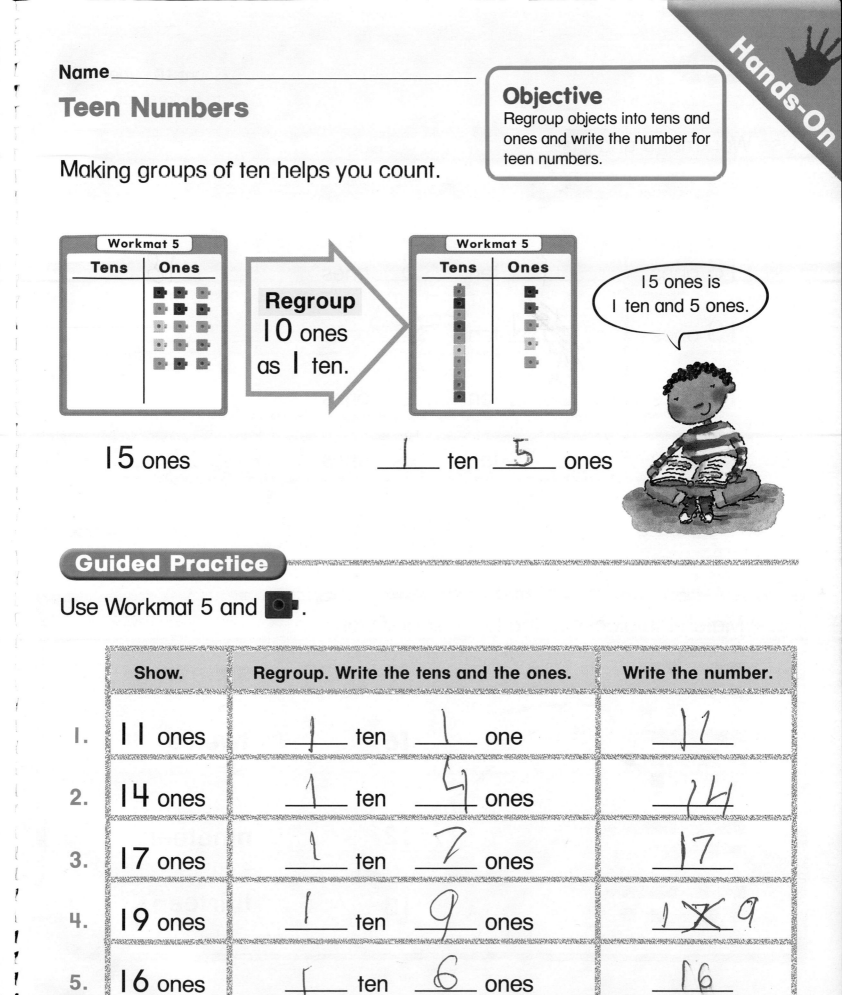

Workmat 5	
Tens	Ones

Regroup 10 ones as 1 ten.

Workmat 5	
Tens	Ones

15 ones is 1 ten and 5 ones.

15 ones   __1__ ten __5__ ones

Guided Practice

Use Workmat 5 and ⬛.

	Show.	Regroup. Write the tens and the ones.	Write the number.
1.	11 ones	__1__ ten __1__ one	11
2.	14 ones	__1__ ten __4__ ones	14
3.	17 ones	__1__ ten __7__ ones	17
4.	19 ones	__1__ ten __9__ ones	1X9
5.	16 ones	__1__ ten __6__ ones	16

Explain Your Thinking What does each digit stand for in 16?

Count 10 cubes
to make 1 ten.

Use Workmat 5 and .

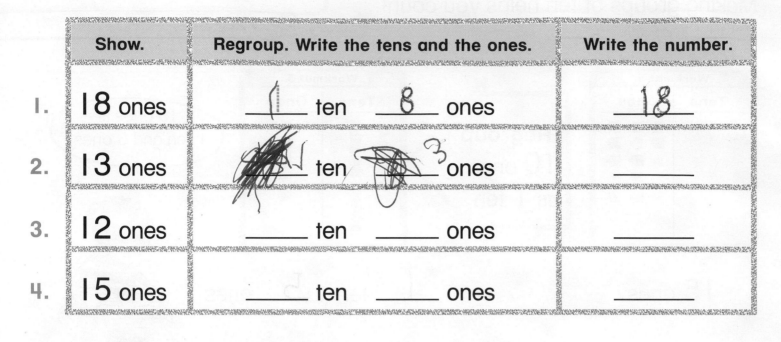

Show.	Regroup. Write the tens and the ones.	Write the number.
1. 18 ones	__1__ ten __8__ ones	__18__
2. 13 ones	~~1~~ ten ~~3~~ 3 ones	____
3. 12 ones	____ ten ____ ones	____
4. 15 ones	__1__ ten ____ ones	____

Reading Math ▶ Vocabulary

5. Match the blocks to the number and word.

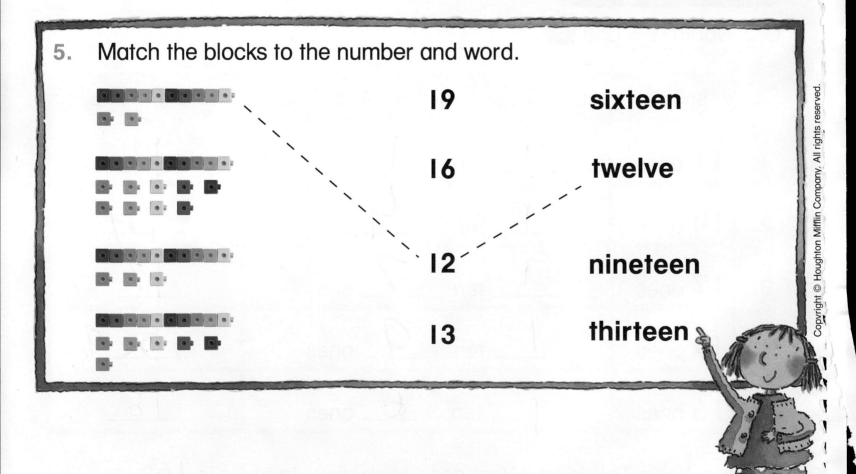

19   sixteen

16   twelve

12   nineteen

13   thirteen

At Home Ask your child to show numbers from this lesson as tens and ones using small objects.

Name_____

Now Try This **Place Value**

To find the value of a digit, find the value of its place.

Count the hundreds, tens, and ones.
Write the hundreds, tens, and ones.
Write the number.

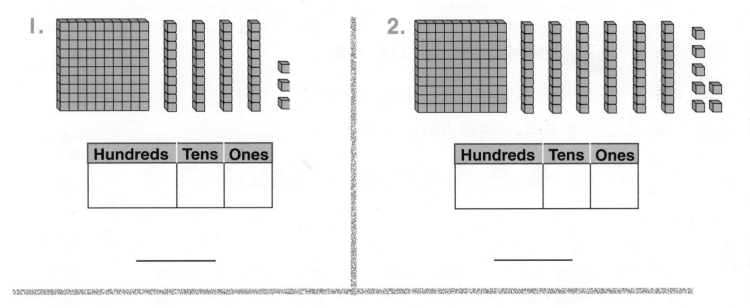

1.

Hundreds	Tens	Ones

_____

2.

Hundreds	Tens	Ones

_____

Circle the value of the red digit.

3. 145

   100   40   5

4. 167

   100   60   7

5. 155

   100   50   5

6. 131

   100   30   1

7. **Talk About It** Explain what each digit stands for in 249.

Math Challenge
Seeing Stars

There are objects in nature
that are star shaped.

This star is found in the ocean. _____

Five seeds make the star in
this fruit that grows on a tree. _____

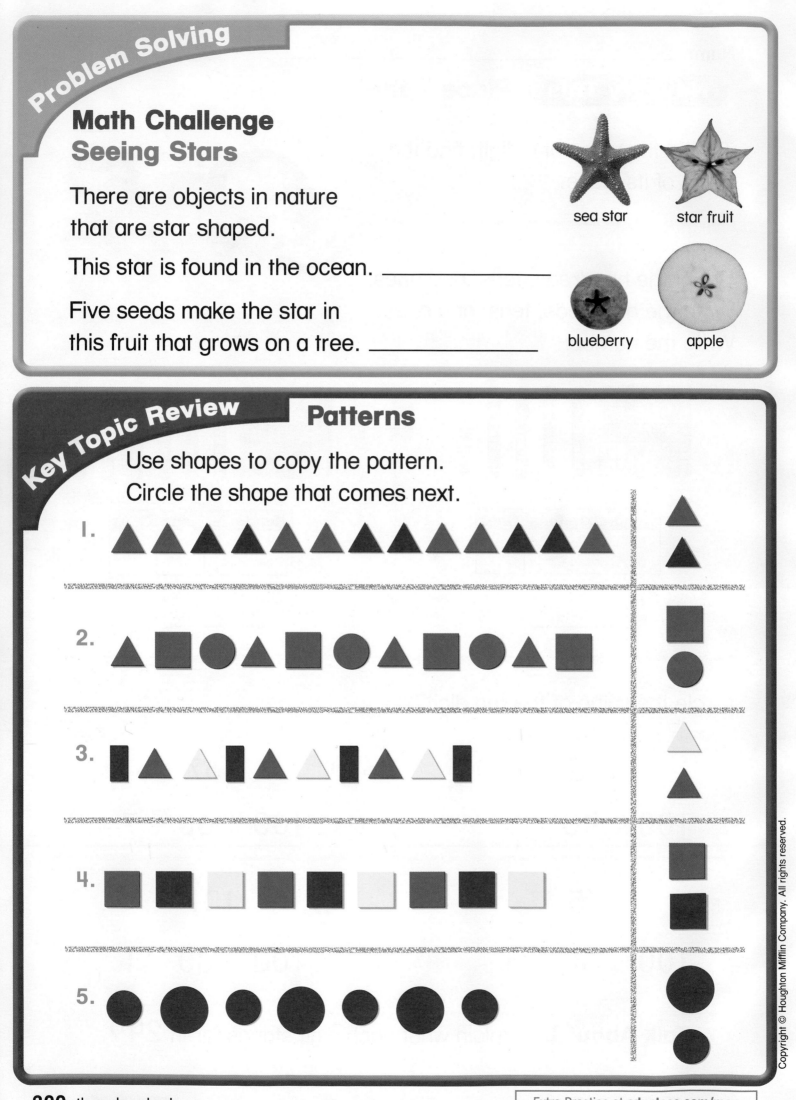

sea star   star fruit

blueberry   apple

Key Topic Review   Patterns

Use shapes to copy the pattern.
Circle the shape that comes next.

1.

2.

3.

4.

5.

Extra Practice at **eduplace.com/map**

Vocabulary

Match the word to the correct statement.

1. **one hundred**   If you have 10 or more ones, you can do this.

2. **regroup**   10 of these equal 1 ten.

3. **tens**   20 ones make 2 of these.

4. **ones**   This is one more than 99.

Concepts and Skills

Write the number of tens shown.
Write the number.

5. _____ tens

_____

thirty

6. _____ tens

_____

sixty

Use Workmat 5 and ▪◻.

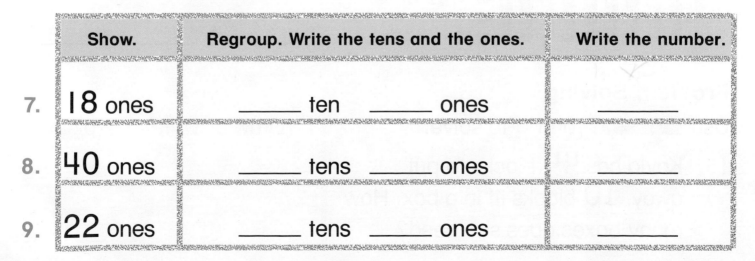

Show.	Regroup. Write the tens and the ones.		Write the number.
7. 18 ones	_____ ten	_____ ones	_____
8. 40 ones	_____ tens	_____ ones	_____
9. 22 ones	_____ tens	_____ ones	_____

Chapter Review/Test

Use Workmat 5, , and ▫ .

Show the number.

Write the number.

10.

Tens	Ones

_____ tens _____ ones _____

thirty-five

11.

Tens	Ones

_____ tens _____ ones _____

fifty-three

Write the tens and the ones. Write the number.

12.

Tens	Ones

_____

forty-eight

13.

Tens	Ones

_____

sixty-two

Write the number in different ways.

14.

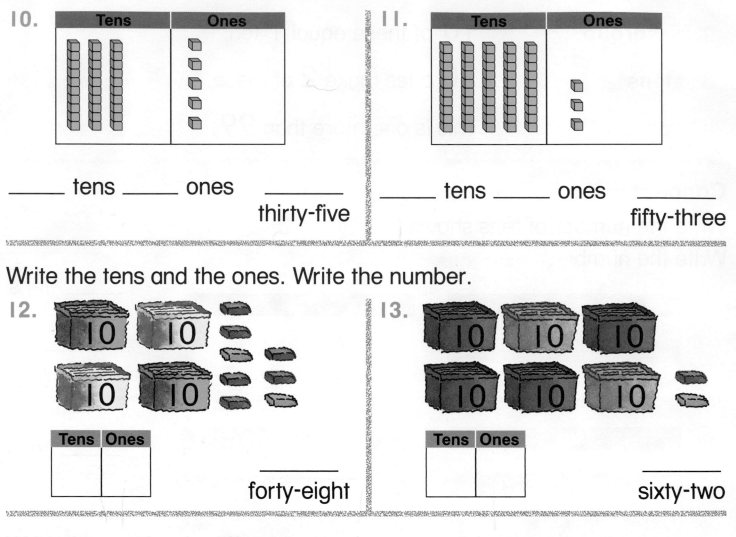

_____ tens _____ ones

_____ + _____ = _____

Problem Solving

Use ⬚⬚⬚ and ▫ to solve.

15. Kayla has 44 blocks to put away. 10 blocks fit in a box. How many boxes does she need?

Draw or write to explain.

_____ boxes

Order and Compare Numbers

INVESTIGATION

Make a graph showing how many ☆ , ♪ ,
and 🐻 there are in the picture.

Home Sweet Home

Find the way home.
Circle the number that is greater
as you move up the path.

50 and 90

26 and 29

50 and 40

75 and 85

83 and 38

10 and 100

65 and 25

32 and 30

71 and 17

47 and 67

Start

Name_____

Order Numbers

A number line can help you write numbers in order.

Number line: 22 23 24 25 26 27 28

22 is just **before** 23.   25 is **between** 24 and 26.   28 is just **after** 27.

Guided Practice

Use the number line.

Number line: 30 31 32 33 34 35 36 37 38 39 40 41 42 43 44 45

Write the number that comes just before.

1. _____, 37

Think
Find 37 on the number line.

2. _____, 43   3. _____, 32

Write the number that comes just after.

4. 44, _____   5. 37, _____   6. 41, _____   7. 30, _____

Write the number that comes between.

8. 39, _____, 41   9. 38, _____, 40   10. 33, _____, 35

Explain Your Thinking Look at Exercise 10. Explain how you know the numbers are in order.

Count forward or backward to find the number.

Use Workmats 7 and 8.

Write the number that comes just before or just after.

1. __87__, 88

2. 91, _____

3. _____, 97

4. _____, 86

5. 99, _____

6. 88, _____

Write the number that comes between.

7. 11, _____, 13

8. 67, _____, 69

9. 28, _____, 30

10. 80, _____, 82

11. 93, _____, 95

12. 45, _____, 47

Write the missing numbers.

Count forward or backward.

13. 55, _____, _____, 58

14. 100, _____, _____, 97

Problem Solving ▶ Number Sense

15. Write the number for the model.

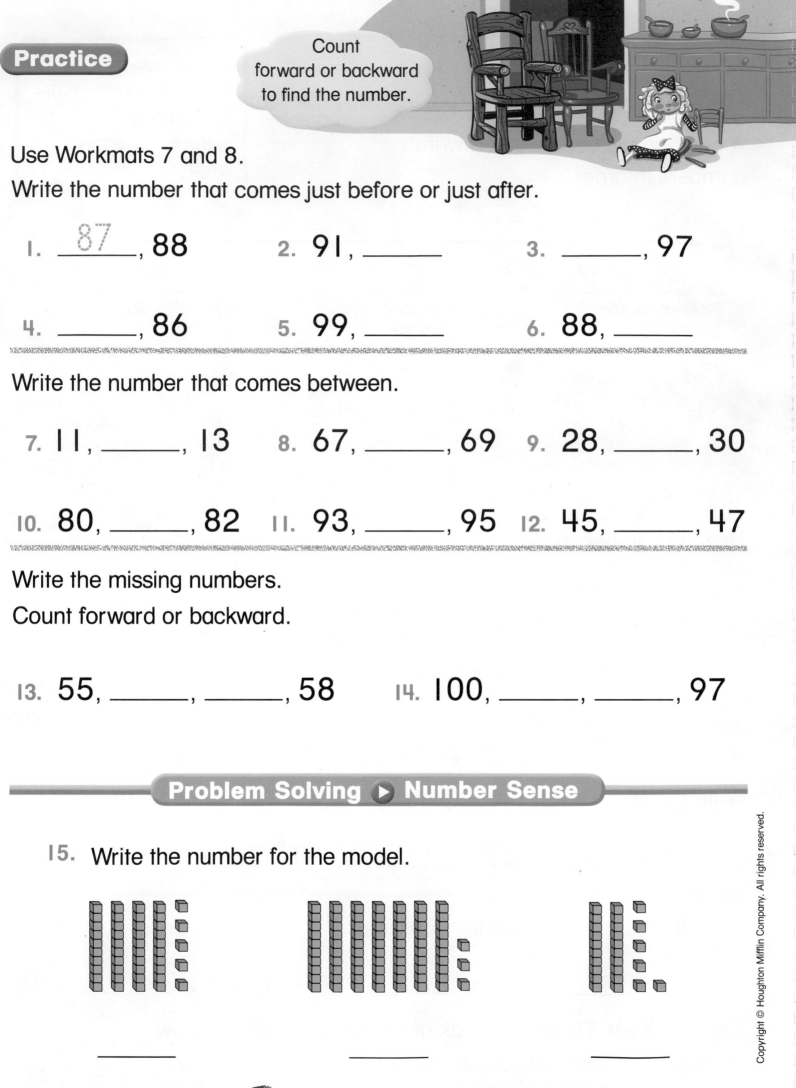

_____   _____   _____

 At Home Write three two-digit numbers. Have your child use the words **before**, **after**, and **between** to tell about the order of the numbers.

Ordinal Numbers

Audio Tutor I/36 Listen and Understand

Some words tell the position of something or someone.

First Second Third Fourth Fifth Sixth Seventh Eighth Ninth Tenth

Guided Practice

Color.

1. third

Think
Count first, second, third.

2. fifth

3. eighth

4. first

5. seventh

6. second

7. sixth

8. ninth

9. fourth

10. seventh

11. tenth

Explain Your Thinking If you are fifth in line, how many people are in front of you?

Color.

Count in order to color the picture.

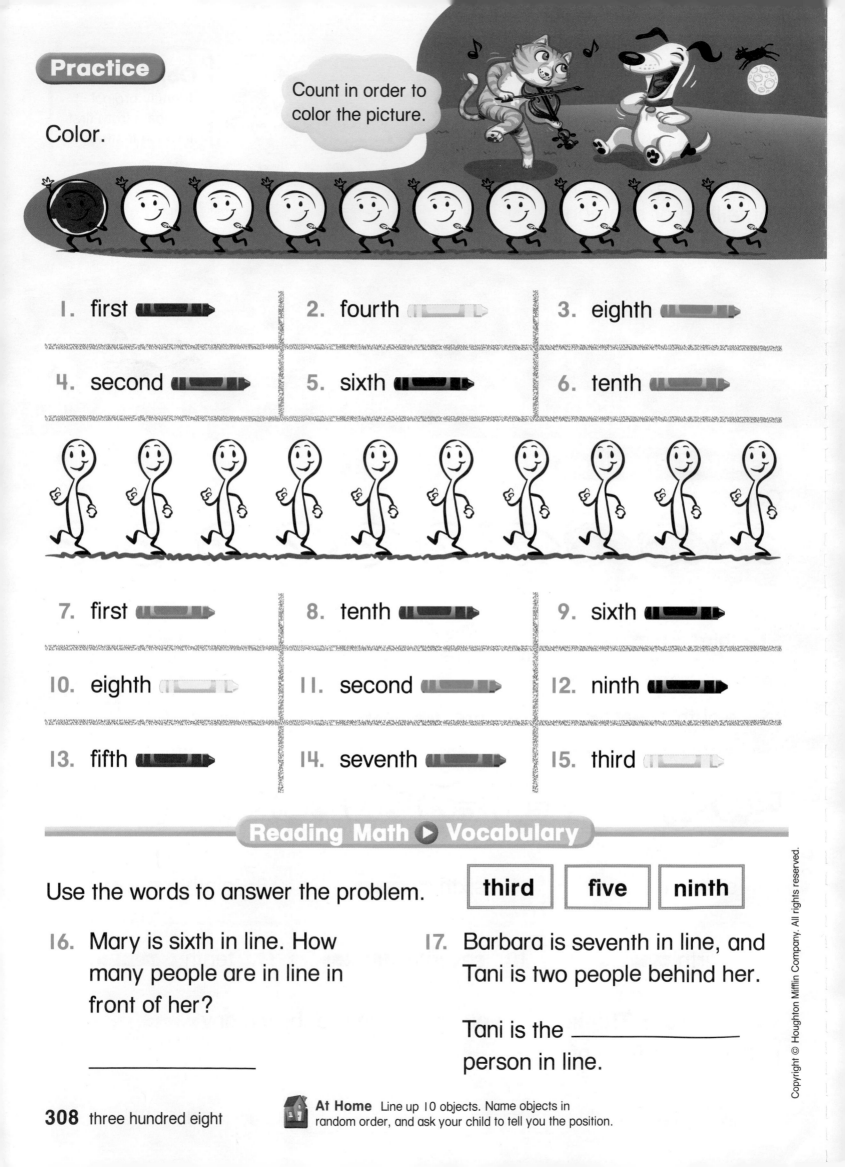

1. first

2. fourth

3. eighth

4. second

5. sixth

6. tenth

7. first

8. tenth

9. sixth

10. eighth

11. second

12. ninth

13. fifth

14. seventh

15. third

Reading Math ▶ Vocabulary

Use the words to answer the problem.

| third | five | ninth |

16. Mary is sixth in line. How many people are in line in front of her?

_____

17. Barbara is seventh in line, and Tani is two people behind her.

Tani is the _____ person in line.

At Home Line up 10 objects. Name objects in random order, and ask your child to tell you the position.

Use Ten to Estimate

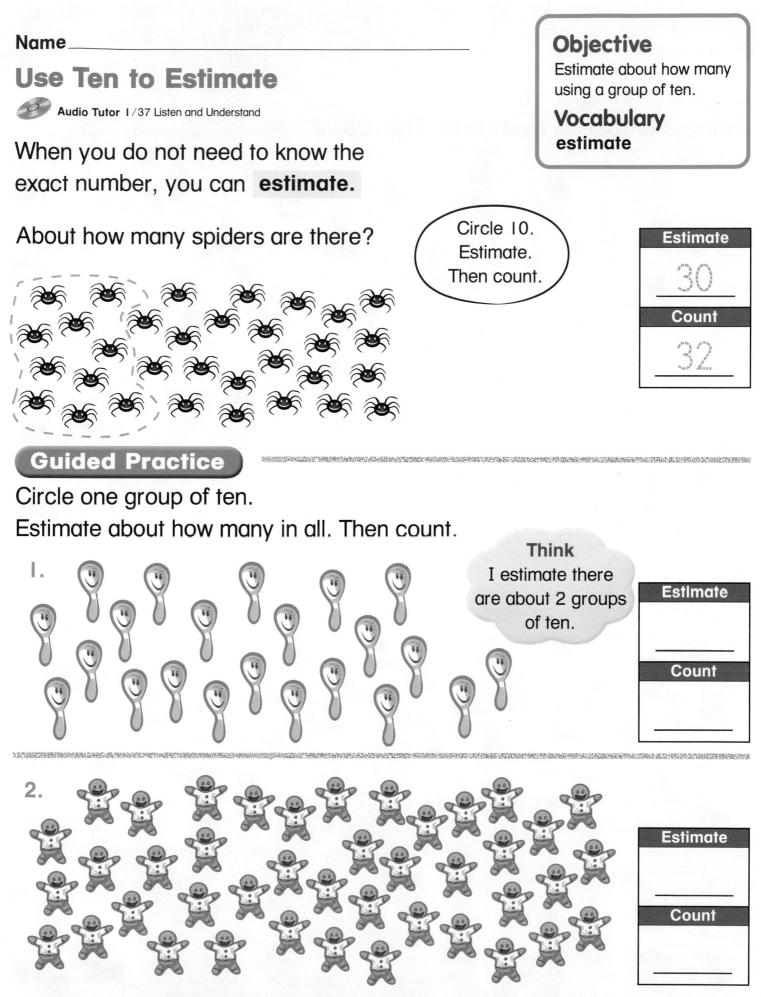

Audio Tutor 1/37 Listen and Understand

Objective
Estimate about how many using a group of ten.
Vocabulary
estimate

When you do not need to know the exact number, you can **estimate.**

About how many spiders are there?

Circle 10.
Estimate.
Then count.

Estimate
30
Count
32

Guided Practice

Circle one group of ten.
Estimate about how many in all. Then count.

Think
I estimate there are about 2 groups of ten.

1.

Estimate
_____
Count
_____

2.

Estimate
_____
Count
_____

Explain Your Thinking Why does it help to circle one group of ten when you estimate?

Remember to use the group of ten to estimate.

Circle one group of ten.
Estimate about how many in all. Then count.

1.

Estimate
20
Count
19

2.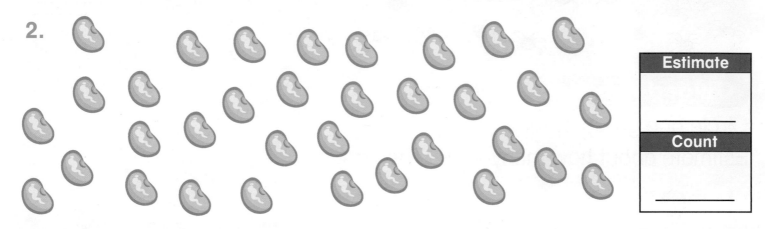

Estimate
_____
Count
_____

3.

Estimate
_____
Count
_____

4.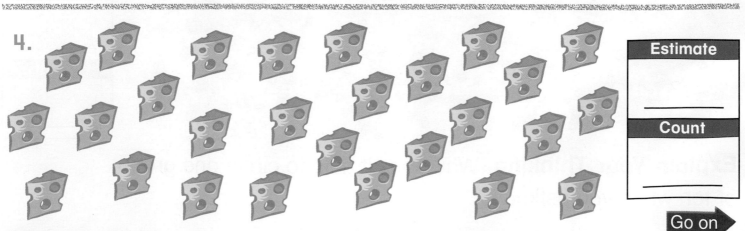

Estimate
_____
Count
_____

Go on ▶

Name_____

Use the graph.

Write how many of each were found.

Shoes Found

5. _____

6. _____

7. _____

Kinds of Shoes

Circle.

8. Which kind of shoe was found the most?

9. Which kind of shoe was found the least?

10. Were there more or ?

11. Were there fewer or ?

12. **Talk About It** What if one more was found? How would the graph change?

  At Home Place 30 to 50 of the same objects in a jar. Show your child 10 of those objects. Ask your child to estimate how many are in there. Then count the objects.

Science Connection
Canada Geese

Canada Geese fly to warm places in the winter. They fly to cool places in the summer. A group of geese is called a flock. Circle the flock of geese that is greater.

flock of **28** geese

flock of **24** geese

Quick Check

Write the number that comes just before.	Write the number that comes just after.	Write the number that comes between.
1. _____, 13	2. 39, _____	3. 77, _____, 79

Find the hat. Color it.

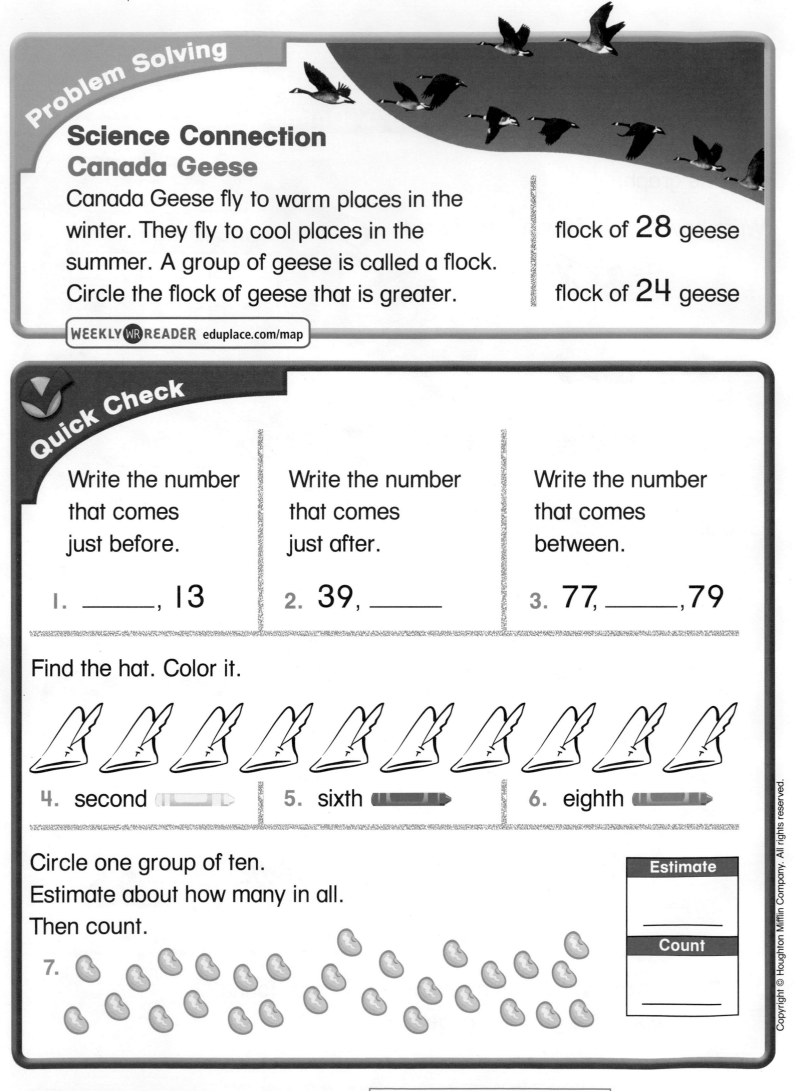

4. second

5. sixth

6. eighth

Circle one group of ten.
Estimate about how many in all.
Then count.

7.

Estimate
_____
Count
_____

Facts Practice, see page 673

Reasonable Answers

Choose the answer that makes sense.

The children in Mr. Reed's class play a game.
Each child takes one handful of 🔲.

**About how many 🔲 can you
pick up in one hand?**

about 10 🔲   about 100 🔲

THINK

DECIDE

Do I need an exact answer?	No. The question asks about how many.
What should I use to solve the problem?	I can use what I know. I know how big a 🔲 is. I know how big my hand is.
Which answer makes more sense?	I can hold about 10 🔲 in my hand. 100 🔲 is too many to hold.

I can pick up about 10 🔲 in one hand.

Estimate.
Circle the answer that makes sense.

Draw or write to explain.

1. Laura takes one handful of pennies. About how many pennies can she hold in one hand?

Think
A penny is this big.

(about **20** pennies)

about **100** pennies

2. Ellis goes to bed after dinner. About how many hours does he sleep at night?

Think
There are 24 hours in a day.

about **8** hours

about **42** hours

Practice

3. Jake's grandfather is the oldest person in his family. About how many years old is his grandfather?

about **6** years old

about **60** years old

4. Berta's dad drives her friends to school. About how many people can fit in his van?

about **10** people

about **85** people

At Home Fill a bowl with items such as cereal or uncooked macaroni. Ask your child to estimate about how many he or she can pick up with one hand. Try it and then count the pieces.

Name_____

Now Try This   **Number Clues**

Use the number line.
Circle the number or numbers that fit the clue.

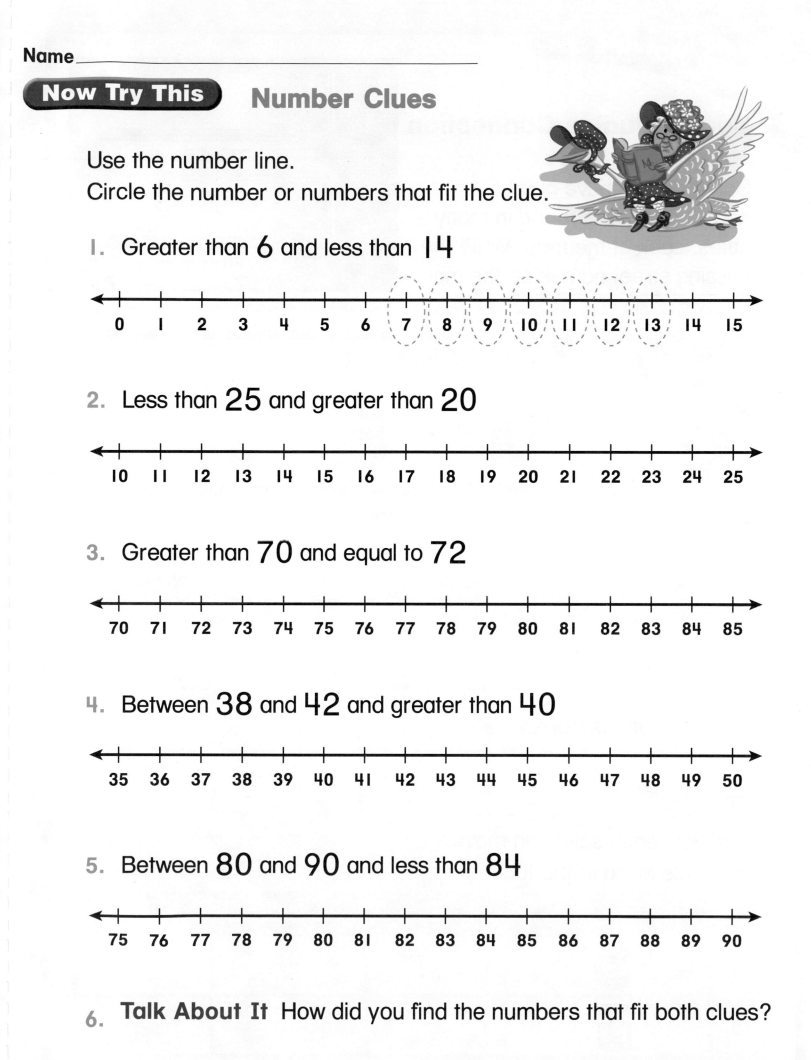

1. Greater than **6** and less than **14**

0 1 2 3 4 5 6 ⟨7 8 9 10 11 12 13⟩ 14 15

2. Less than **25** and greater than **20**

10 11 12 13 14 15 16 17 18 19 20 21 22 23 24 25

3. Greater than **70** and equal to **72**

70 71 72 73 74 75 76 77 78 79 80 81 82 83 84 85

4. Between **38** and **42** and greater than **40**

35 36 37 38 39 40 41 42 43 44 45 46 47 48 49 50

5. Between **80** and **90** and less than **84**

75 76 77 78 79 80 81 82 83 84 85 86 87 88 89 90

6. **Talk About It** How did you find the numbers that fit both clues?

Social Studies Connection
Number Streets

Some streets have number names. They are found in many cities. Look at the map. Write the missing street names on the map.

Third Street

First Street

WEEKLY WR READER eduplace.com/map

Key Topic Review

Solid Shapes

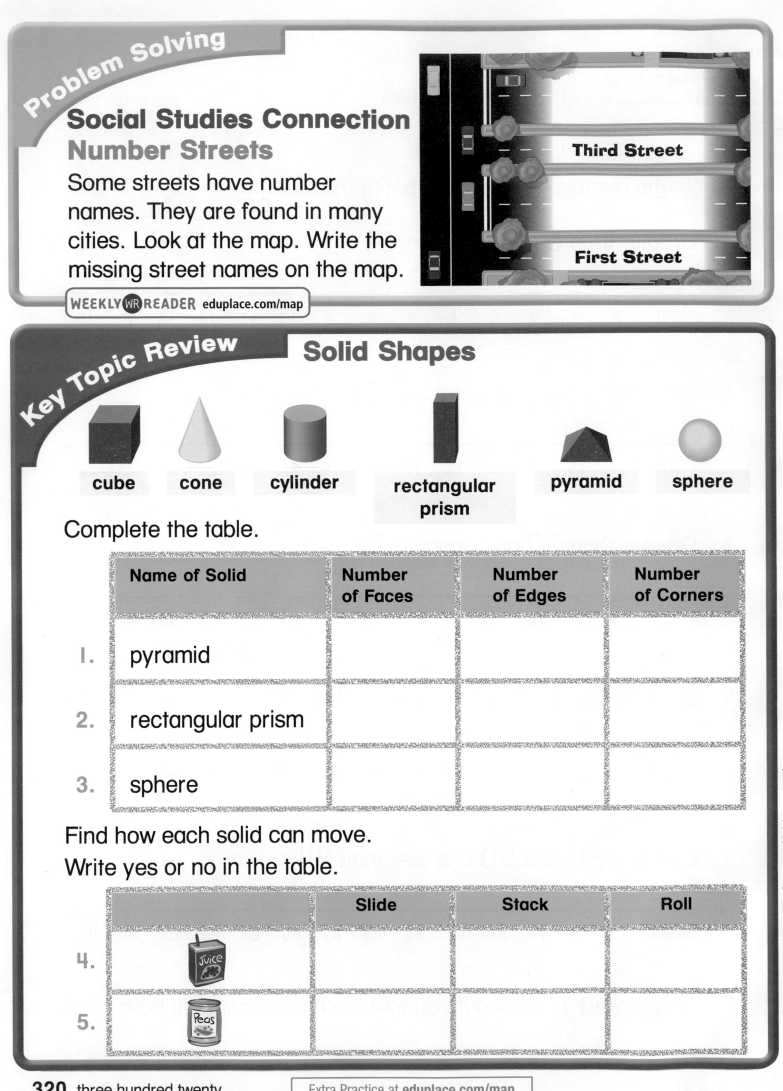

cube   cone   cylinder   rectangular prism   pyramid   sphere

Complete the table.

	Name of Solid	Number of Faces	Number of Edges	Number of Corners
1.	pyramid			
2.	rectangular prism			
3.	sphere			

Find how each solid can move.
Write yes or no in the table.

		Slide	Stack	Roll
4.	Juice			
5.	Peas			

Extra Practice at **eduplace.com/map**

Vocabulary

Complete the sentence.

| less than |
| equal to |
| after |

1. 60 is _____ 60.

2. 19 comes just _____ 18.

3. 37 is _____ 47.

Concepts and Skills

Use Workmats 7 and 8.
Write the number that comes just before or just after.

4. ____, 71   5. 62, ____   6. ____, 80

Write the number that comes between.

7. 13, ____, 15   8. 31, ____, 33   9. 64, ____, 66

Color.

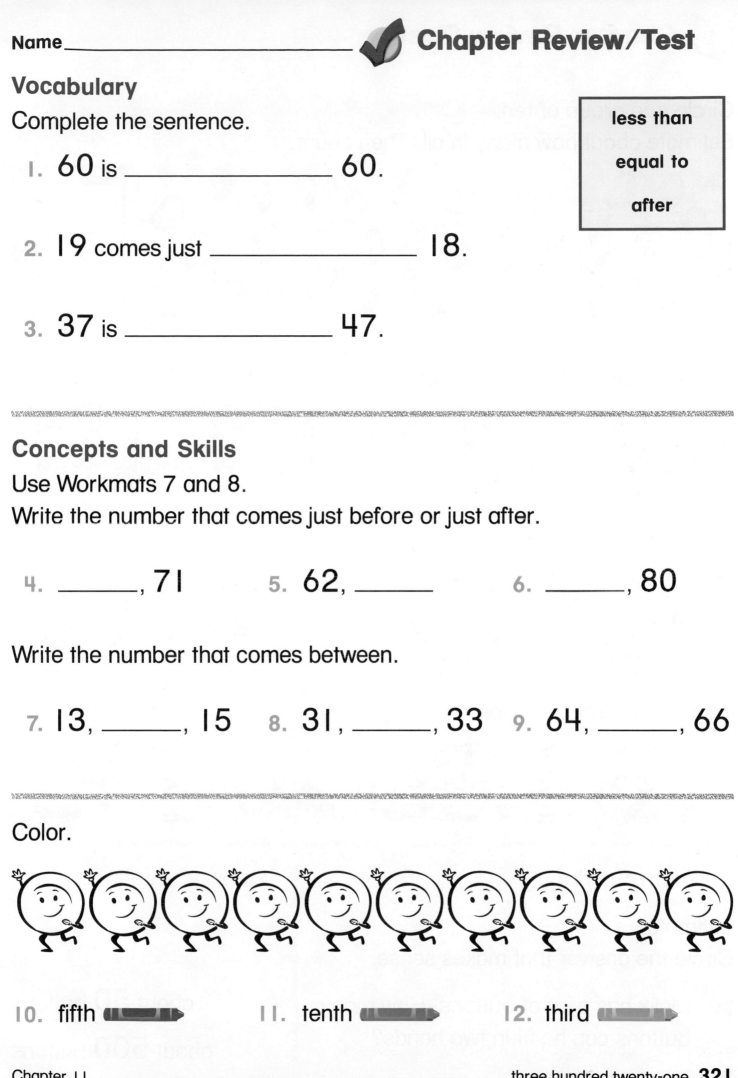

10. fifth ◀▬▬▶   11. tenth ◀▬▬▶   12. third ◀▬▬▶

Circle one group of ten.

Estimate about how many in all. Then count.

13.

Estimate
_____
Count
_____

Circle the number that is greater.

14. 45 54

15. 86 87

Circle the number that is less.

16. 24 34

17. 92 29

Compare. Circle >, <, or =.

18.  29 > < = 29

19. 46 > < = 52

Problem Solving

Draw or write to explain.

Estimate.

Circle the answer that makes sense.

20. Malik has a jar of buttons. How many buttons can he fit in two hands?

about **50** buttons

about **500** buttons

Number Patterns

CHAPTER 12

INVESTIGATION

What patterns do you see?

✔️ Painted Post

Skip count by **2**s to find how many posts there are in the fence.

Use  to color in every other post.

Name_____

Count by Twos

To **skip count** by 2s, count two at a time.

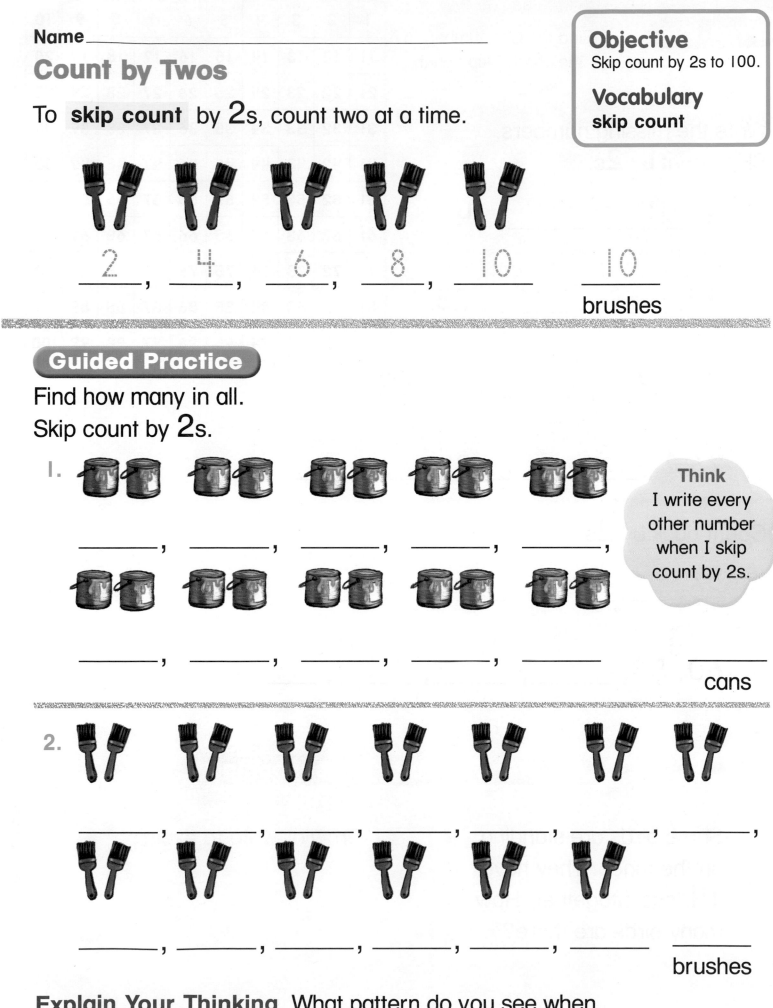

_2_ , _4_ , _6_ , _8_ , _10_   _10_
                                       brushes

Guided Practice

Find how many in all.
Skip count by 2s.

1.

Think
I write every other number when I skip count by 2s.

_____ , _____ , _____ , _____ , _____ ,

_____ , _____ , _____ , _____ , _____
                                              cans

2.

_____ , _____ , _____ , _____ , _____ , _____ , _____ ,

_____ , _____ , _____ , _____ , _____
                                              brushes

Explain Your Thinking What pattern do you see when
you skip count by 2s?

Find the first number on the chart. Skip count.

1	2	3	4	5	6	7	8	9	10
11	12	13	14	15	16	17	18	19	20
21	22	23	24	25	26	27	28	29	30
31	32	33	34	35	36	37	38	39	40
41	42	43	44	45	46	47	48	49	50
51	52	53	54	55	56	57	58	59	60
61	62	63	64	65	66	67	68	69	70
71	72	73	74	75	76	77	78	79	80
81	82	83	84	85	86	87	88	89	90
91	92	93	94	95	96	97	98	99	100

Write the missing numbers.
Skip count by 2s.

1. 8, __10__, __12__, 14

2. 22, _____, _____, 28

3. 54, 56, _____, _____, 62

4. 76, _____, _____, 82, _____, _____

Count back by 2s.

5. 26, _____, _____, _____, _____, 16

6. 60, 58, _____, _____, _____, _____

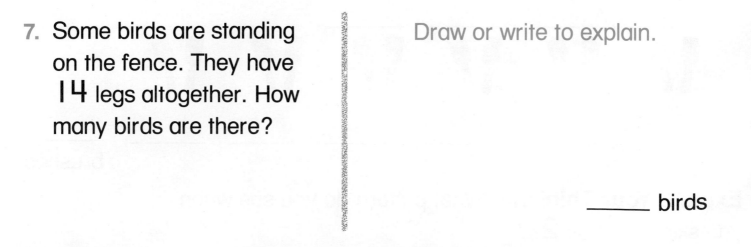

Problem Solving ▶ Reasoning

7. Some birds are standing on the fence. They have 14 legs altogether. How many birds are there?

Draw or write to explain.

_____ birds

 At Home Have your child skip count by 2s to find the number of spoons in the kitchen.

Count by Fives

To skip count by 5s, count five at a time.

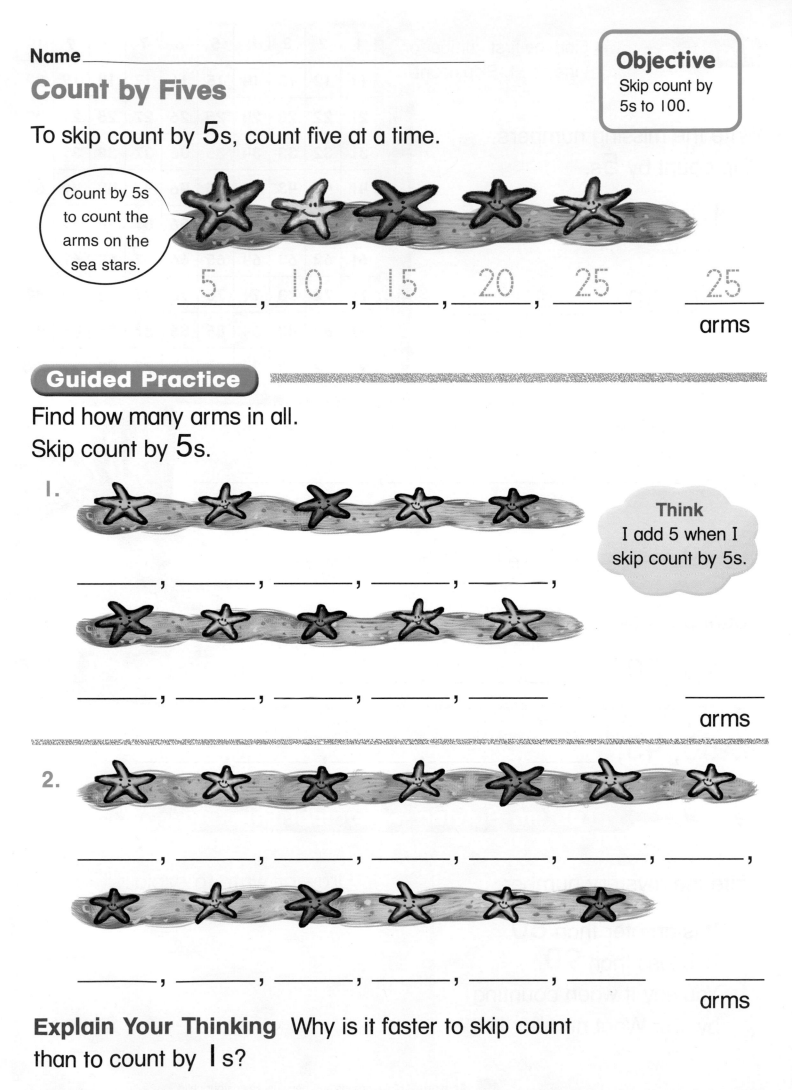

Count by 5s to count the arms on the sea stars.

5 , 10 , 15 , 20 , 25   25
arms

Guided Practice

Find how many arms in all.
Skip count by 5s.

1.

Think
I add 5 when I skip count by 5s.

____ , ____ , ____ , ____ , ____ ,

____ , ____ , ____ , ____   ____
arms

2.

____ , ____ , ____ , ____ , ____ , ____ , ____ ,

____ , ____ , ____ , ____ , ____   ____
arms

Explain Your Thinking Why is it faster to skip count than to count by 1s?

Find the first number on the chart. Skip count.

1	2	3	4	5	6	7	8	9	10
11	12	13	14	15	16	17	18	19	20
21	22	23	24	25	26	27	28	29	30
31	32	33	34	35	36	37	38	39	40
41	42	43	44	45	46	47	48	49	50
51	52	53	54	55	56	57	58	59	60
61	62	63	64	65	66	67	68	69	70
71	72	73	74	75	76	77	78	79	80
81	82	83	84	85	86	87	88	89	90
91	92	93	94	95	96	97	98	99	100

Write the missing numbers.
Skip count by **5**s.

1. 10, 15, _20_ , _25_

2. 25, 30, ____, ____

3. 60, ____, ____, 75

4. 35, ____, ____, ____, ____, ____

5. 75, ____, ____, 90, ____, ____

Count back by **5**s.

6. 25, 20, ____, ____, ____, 0

7. 50, 45, ____, ____, ____, ____, ____

Problem Solving ▶ Logical Thinking

Write the mystery number.

8. It is greater than **80**.
   It is less than **90**.
   You say it when counting
   by **5**s. What number is it?

   _____

Draw or write to explain.

 At Home Make groups of 5 pennies. Have your child skip count by 5s to find the number of pennies in all.

More Than, Less Than

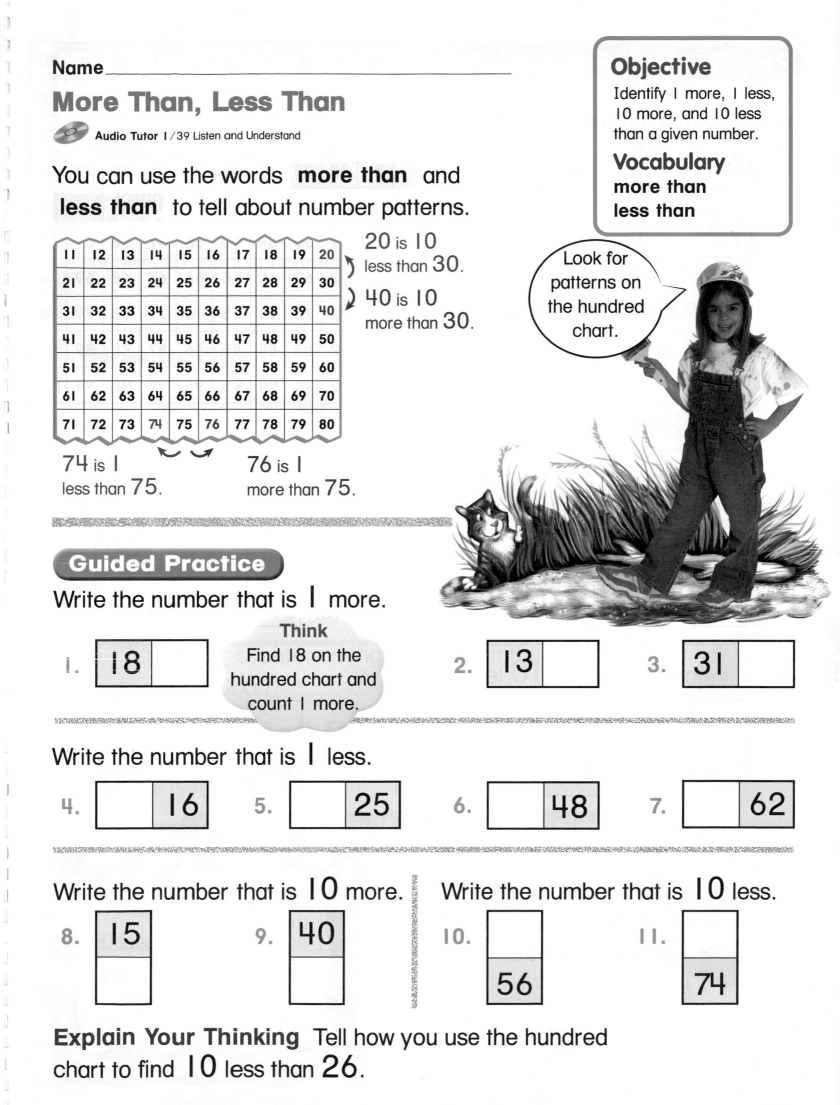

Audio Tutor 1/39 Listen and Understand

Objective
Identify 1 more, 1 less, 10 more, and 10 less than a given number.

Vocabulary
more than
less than

You can use the words **more than** and **less than** to tell about number patterns.

11	12	13	14	15	16	17	18	19	20
21	22	23	24	25	26	27	28	29	30
31	32	33	34	35	36	37	38	39	40
41	42	43	44	45	46	47	48	49	50
51	52	53	54	55	56	57	58	59	60
61	62	63	64	65	66	67	68	69	70
71	72	73	74	75	76	77	78	79	80

20 is 10 less than 30.

40 is 10 more than 30.

74 is 1 less than 75.

76 is 1 more than 75.

Look for patterns on the hundred chart.

Guided Practice

Write the number that is 1 more.

Think Find 18 on the hundred chart and count 1 more.

1. | 18 | |

2. | 13 | |

3. | 31 | |

Write the number that is 1 less.

4. | | 16 |

5. | | 25 |

6. | | 48 |

7. | | 62 |

Write the number that is 10 more.

8. | 15 |
   | |

9. | 40 |
   | |

Write the number that is 10 less.

10. | |
    | 56 |

11. | |
    | 74 |

Explain Your Thinking Tell how you use the hundred chart to find 10 less than 26.

Music Connection
Counting Notes

This is one type of note. ♪

A note is a symbol used for writing music. A beat is a way to count when singing music. In some songs, 2 notes make one beat. How many notes are in 8 beats? Skip count by 2s.

♫ ♫ ♫ ♫ ♫ ♫ ♫ ♫

____ ____ ____ ____ ____ ____ ____ ____

_____ notes

Pictograph

How Children Ride to School

🚌	� � � � � �
🚲	� �
🚗	� � � �

Key: Each � stands for 1 child

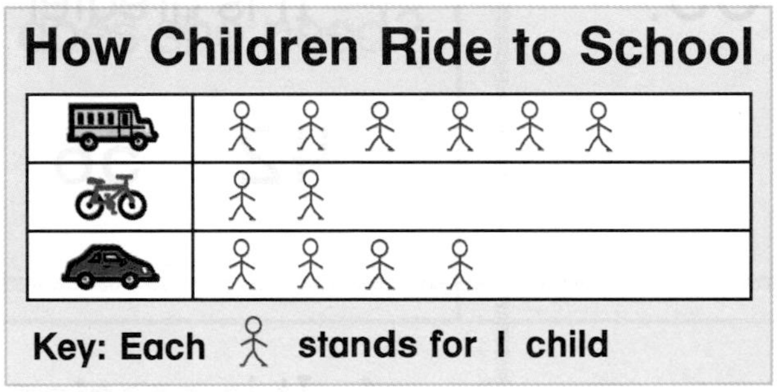

Use the pictograph.

1. How many children ride 🚌 ?

   _____ children

2. How many children ride 🚲 ?

   _____ children

3. Which way do fewer children ride?

   🚌   🚗

2. How do most children get to school?

   🚌   🚲   🚗

Extra Practice at **eduplace.com/map**

Vocabulary

Complete the sentence.

skip count
odd
more than

1. 37 is 10 _____ 27.

2. If I cannot make equal groups,

   it is an _____ number.

3. When I count by 2s I _____.

Concepts and Skills

Write the missing numbers.
Skip count by 2s.

4. 40, 42, _____, _____, 48, _____

5. 90, _____, 94, _____, _____, 100

Write the missing numbers.
Skip count by 5s.

6. 20, 25, _____, _____, _____

7. 80, _____, _____, _____, _____

Write the number that is 1 more or 1 less.

8. | | 19 |
   |---|---|

9. | 57 | |
   |---|---|

10. | | 73 |
    |---|---|

11. | | 52 |
    |---|---|

Write the number that is 10 more or 10 less.

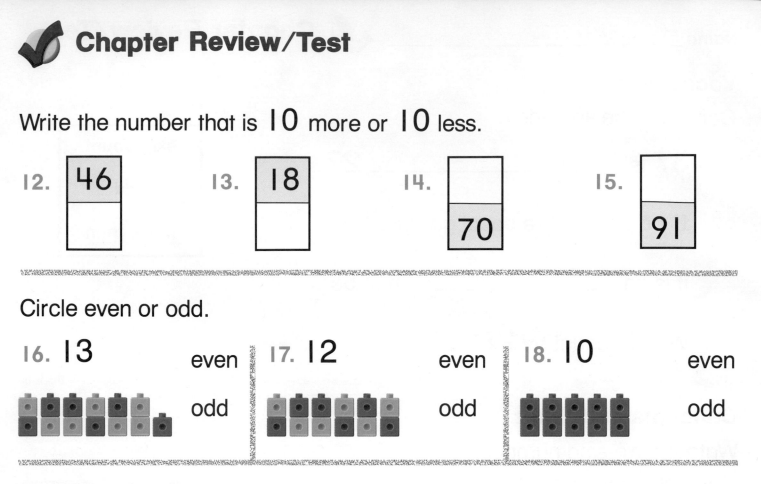

12. | 46 |
    |----|
    | |

13. | 18 |
    |----|
    | |

14. | |
    |----|
    | 70 |

15. | |
    |----|
    | 91 |

Circle even or odd.

16. 13   even

                odd

17. 12   even

                odd

18. 10   even

                odd

Problem Solving

Find the pattern.
Solve.

19. Katie writes 2 stories a week. How many stories will she write by the end of 5 weeks?

1 week	2 weeks	3 weeks	4 weeks	5 weeks
2				

_____ stories

20. Kyle has 5 patches. He earns 5 more patches a month. How many patches will he have by the end of 4 months?

Start	1 month	2 months	3 months	4 months
5				

_____ patches

Name_____

Putting Numbers in Order

1. Write the numbers in order from least to greatest.

   48 23 17

   ____ ____ ____

2. Write the numbers in order from greatest to least.

   36 66 50

   ____ ____ ____

3. Tim drops these cards. Write the numbers in order from greatest to least.

   59 18 80

   ____ ____ ____

4. Draw a line from each set to the number that has the same value.

   65

   13

   41

   Write the numbers in order from least to greatest.

   ____ ____ ____

Calculator
Skip Count

Use 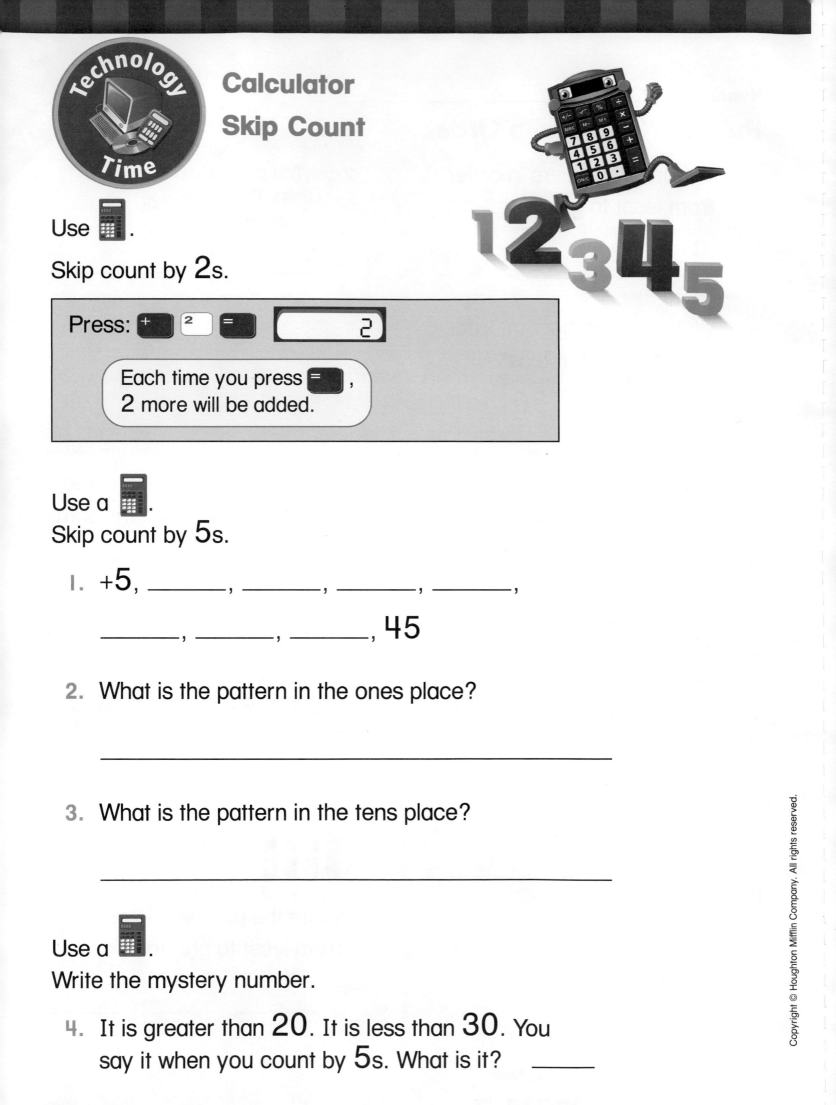 .

Skip count by 2s.

Press: [+] [2] [=]   2

Each time you press [=],
2 more will be added.

Use a ▣ .
Skip count by 5s.

1. +5, _____, _____, _____, _____,

   _____, _____, _____, 45

2. What is the pattern in the ones place?

   _____

3. What is the pattern in the tens place?

   _____

Use a ▣ .
Write the mystery number.

4. It is greater than 20. It is less than 30. You
   say it when you count by 5s. What is it? _____

Vocabulary

Complete the sentence.

	estimate
	less than

1. 67 is _____ 76.

2. To find about how many, you can _____.

Concepts and Skills

Write the tens and the ones.
Write the number.

3.

Tens	Ones

_____

4.

Tens	Ones

_____

Write the number in different ways.

5.

_____ tens _____ ones

_____ + _____ = _____

Use Workmats 7 and 8.

Write the number that comes between.

6. 35, _____, 37   7. 92, _____, 94   8. 18, _____, 20

Compare. Circle >, <, or =.

9. 67 > < = 69

10. 92 > < = 92

✔ Unit 4 Test

Color.

11. tenth   12. first   13. eighth

Write the missing numbers.
Skip count by 2s.

14. 60, 62, _____, _____   15. 48, _____, 52, _____

Write the missing numbers.
Skip count by 5s.

16. 15, _____, _____, 30   17. 65, _____, 75, _____

Circle even or odd.

18. 15

even

odd

19. 18

even

odd

Problem Solving

Use ▭▭▭▭▭▭▭▭▭▭ and ▭ to solve.

Draw or write to explain.

20. Sam sews 43 buttons in rows. 10 buttons fit in each row. How many rows does he sew?

_____ rows

Test-Taking Tips

Check your work when you have finished all the problems.

Reread each problem to make sure you have answered the question.

Multiple Choice

Fill in the ○ for the correct answer.

1. How many tens are in 79?

6   7   8   9
○   ○   ○   ○

3. Which is the third boat?

○   ○   ○   ○

2. Choose a sign to make the sentence true.

24 ◯ 36

<   >   =   +
○   ○   ○   ○

4. Mark the shape that shows fourths.

○   ○   ○   ○

Multiple Choice

Fill in the ○ for the correct answer. NH means Not Here.

5. How many faces are on this solid?

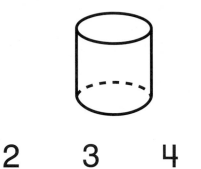

2	3	4	5
○	○	○	○

6. Which number is between **56** and **58**?

55	57	59	60
○	○	○	○

7. Which number does this show?

34	43	46	NH
○	○	○	○

Open Response

Solve.

8. Write the missing numbers. Skip count by **5**s.

20, _____, _____, 35, _____

9. Tomas has **10** nickels, **5** pennies, and **3** dimes in his bank. If he takes out one coin without looking, what coin will it probably be?

_____

10. Which numbers are even numbers?

33   34   35   36   37

_____ and _____

Education Place

Look for Cumulative Test Prep at
eduplace.com/**map** for more practice.

UNIT 5

The Tortoise The and the Hare and the Race Again

written by Laura Black
illustrated by Greg Scheetz

READING MATH

Race Time

Look back at the story to answer these questions.

● 1. Did the race end in the morning or evening?

● 2. Who took a longer time to finish the race?

■ 3. If Hare finished the race 1 hour after Tortoise, what time would it be?

▲ 4. Show this time on both clocks.

3 o'clock

Answers

1. evening   2. Hare   3. 7:00   4.

3:00

Reading Strategies

● Draw Conclusions
● Compare and Contrast
■ Infer
▲ Noting Details

8

The race is beginning.
Here are the rules.
Bike over the mountain
and swim through the pool.
Then put on your helmet,
your kneepads, and skates.
Skate to the finish line
and you'll win the race!

What time is it?

Tortoise crosses the finish line
with time to spare.
Slow and steady won the race—
will someone wake up Hare?

What time is it?

Tortoise must speed up!

An hour has passed.
While Hare races forward,
poor Tortoise is last.

What time is it?

START

Hare sees the finish line
from his spot by the tree.
With so little time left,
he thinks he's home free!

What time is it?

FINISH

ZZZZZZ

3

It has been two hours
since this race began.
Tortoise climbs to the top,
while Hare rests in the sand.

What time is it?

Another hour has passed.
Hare puts on his gear.
Tortoise is still swimming—
he's not even near.

What time is it?